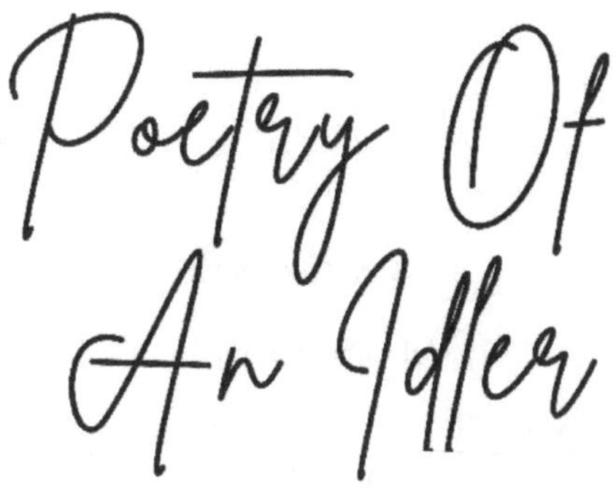
Poetry Of
An Idler

AF534781

S. K. GARG

BlueRose ONE.com
Stories Matter

First Published in March 2023

**ISBN: 978-93-5704-422-6**

**BLUEROSE PUBLISHERS**
www.BlueRoseONE.com
info@bluerosepublishers.com
+91 8882 898 898

**Cover Design:**
Muskan Sachdeva

**Typographic Design:**
Pooja Sharma

**Distributed by:** BlueRose, Amazon, Flipkart

Poetry of -

# *An Idler*

**S.K. Garg**

Principal

+91- 6264976849

*"An idler is, he who sits still and contemplates"*

# Dedication

I dedicate this poetry of mine to my late dear wife ***"Krishna"*** whom I loved dearly and still love her in the form of my dear companion soul.

Physically, she is no more; she walks in the heavens; she comes and goes to make a bridge between herself and mine.

Thus, two loving souls and two atoms combine to form a divine molecule that will rejoice and reign in the heavens, and in the extreme, we will get salvation.

**– S. K. Garg**

# Forewords

Poetry is the music of an aching soul, we hear in the breaths of a poet. Ache bitter or sweet, it's the only ache which compels him to sing from the lamentation to the rapture.

The creation of the Universe, poetry itself, is the result of the sudden ache within the divinity. So is the art of an artist and the poetry of the poet. Here, the ache is within and without – the inner ache takes the harmony with that of the outer and thus a poet wanders from Abyss to the Everest, Shark to the Lark and Dust to the Diana.

I am not a Scholar nor a person known among the people but exactly an idler perfect who sits still and alone, and thinks – When, Why, What, Where, Who and How? And I get the answer too in the silver silence.

There is nothing except the ache – the whole universe is aching and I think that this great ache is 'MAYA' itself – the impulse of the creation, an art divine of the creator. Do you wish to hear its melody? Let me sit still on the grass and Lo, here is the poetry of an Idler.

**– Author**

**S. K. Garg**

# Contents


**Love** ..... 1

Two Beating Hearts On Wedding ..... 2

Two Beating Hearts At The Time Of Valediction ..... 6

Two Beating Hearts At Different Poles ..... 10

Two Beating Hearts In The Hope Of Union ..... 14

Two Beating Hearts After Long Valediction ..... 18

Fear And Frown In Love ..... 22

Blow, Blow O' Winds! ..... 23

Love Never Dies ..... 24

I Hate You Sparrow ..... 25

Nectar Of Lovers ..... 26

**Meta-Physics** ..... 27

The Crossing ..... 28

Misery of a Pond ..... 45

Pleasure Of An Idler ..... 47

I Fear, Lest I Become A Millionaire ..... 49

The Cloud ..... 51

On A Rainy Evening ..... 55

To The Storm ..... 57

To The Eternity.....59

To The Sovereign.....61

To The Solitudes.....63

Adam's Letter To The God.....65

When I Sit Alone.....67

The Labyrinth.....69

Tear'd Mutes.....71

An Embryonic Dream.....72

I Weep For You, O' Poor Creatures!.....74

Insecta.....76

Wounded Dove – The Woman.....77

A Child And The Crust.....79

The Golden Cage And The Bird.....82

Dear Son Of God.....84

A Wounded Dog.....86

Under Shivering Stars.....88

How Falls The Night In A Countryside.....91

A Pair Of Dove.....92

An Old Woman – Cow Dung Collector.....96

O' Shelley, Thy Lark Is Breathing Its Last.....98

**Miscellaneous** ........................................................ 102

On Playing Badminton ........................................................ 103

To The Sky ........................................................ 104

On Melancholy ........................................................ 106

Verse, O' Verse! ........................................................ 108

The Oasis ........................................................ 110

To The Poetic Muse ........................................................ 112

On Talking To The Portrait Of My Love ........................................................ 113

Spectrum Of Religion ........................................................ 114

Lines Written In 1993 ........................................................ 115

Doctors From Chancer To Present ........................................................ 116

Melpomene ........................................................ 117

Lines Written In February 2009 ........................................................ 119

On The Path Of Lover ........................................................ 121

The Creator ........................................................ 130

Lines Written On The Eve Of Retirement ........................................................ 133

My Dear Companion Soul ........................................................ 134

# Love

"Lover mundane in the mundanity,
Seek thy shelter,
I seeker of the beauty."

"O Beauty to the seeker of the truth,
thy whispers can utter whole of it."

# Two Beating Hearts On Wedding

## I

O' Virgin! I remember that evening,
Colourful calm and quiet,
Amid flowers sweet-scented,
Bright red and white.

I like an insect
Attracted towards your petalous cheeks,
Among murmur and whisper
Of birds and bees.

Attracted towards your winy eyes,
Oval neck white breast.
Curly hair like nice ebony –
My treasure, my heart's feast.

When enchanted like a Serpant bright,
It was love at the first sight.

– (December' 1980)

## II

Day and night, night and day
In sleep or sound, on the bed or on the way
Amid madding crowd or in a solitude
I dreamt of you, O' powerful nymph.

In the sun, in the moon, in the stary sky,
In the swing of rainbow swinging high.
In fields, in flowers, in beautiful lawns,
In parks and gardens at sunset and dawn.

I madly wandered for the sake of you,
For the sake of you, O' virgin true.
For the sake of peace, for the sake of beauty,
Neglecting my duty.

I wandered O' fair nymph,
My goal, my claim, my triumph

– (December' 1980)

## III

We, two bodies one soul, two brains one fancy,
Two paths one goal, in the seasons of Nancy.
On velvet green, under fresh full moon,
Expanding our arms to embrace us soon.

We came nearer – two beating hearts,
Lips with lips, our palmy arms.
What unique we felt,
Ah! Our bodies melt.

Sleeping buds open'd their eyes,
Sweet smell did spread in the earth and sky.
New life they found your chased breasts,
Your face appear'd like sun in the east.

We laid calm breathing clasping arms,
Our faces were red and breaths warm.

– (December' 1980)

## IV

The day of our wedding – The Loveliest day,
Come, come, O' Darling – our fortune's day.

Like a swirling river runs oceanward,
Full of youth delight and mirth,
With zeal, with glory and the pride,
Merges it's all and falls in the wide.

I embraced her youth, her beating heart,
Like a moon in the sky with a cloud smart.
She murmured something – her love essence,
And clinge to my heart – a dove innocent.

Our fingers were moving on each other's head,
Like Cupid and the psyche we seemed on the bed.
Each pulse and beat was reminding our days,
Virtue of love, its power and ways.

– (December' 1980)

# Two Beating Hearts At The Time Of Valediction

## I

Parting kiss O' belle!
Till our hearts beat together.
And strikes the silence,
Our combined murmur.

Till finds the shelter,
My weary heart.
In the pleasant shadow,
Of thy hair – my guard.

And we feel – sensation sweet,
In the blissful showers.
When mingle our whispers,
In the season of flowers.

Why stand statuesque, why mourn,
Why answer not, O' delicate born!

– (February' 1981)

## II

Abhor not valediction,
Be cheer, O' Beauty!
Diana resides on thy lips,
Welcome not the mournful Deity.

Valediction – lovers bid adieu,
To each other.
But forget not, yes, forget not,
It makes love stronger.

Adore Valediction,
For the pleasure of union.
When you and I will meet together,
Like creeper with the Bunyan

Still tear'd, thy tears weaken me, O' belle!
What I see, your face turned Pale!

– (February' 1981)

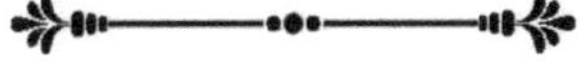

## III

Sun hides in the horizon,
When goes abroad.
And pervades the gloom,
In the nature broad.

Poor creeper – deprived of the warmth,
Of her dear.
Sighs in the dark,
And shed tear.

No fickle but full of fancy,
The tear'd mute with eyes torn.
Gazes the path of her lover –
The Mourn.

And dazzling sun when appears,
Her heart joys and he wipes her tears.

– (February' 1981)

## IV

Parting kiss O' beau!
Till we meet further.
With heart beating frequent,
Embracing each other.

Till finds the shelter,
My weary heart.
In the pleasant shadow,
Of the eyebrows – my guard.

And we feel the pleasure of union,
After long valediction.
When pale lips water each other,
After hours of dejection.

Flow of tears – it's nature born,
Flow in rapid till comes the morn.

– (February' 1981)

## Two Beating Hearts At Different Poles

### I

When drops of the midnight dew,
Slowly trickle on the earth.
Through the flowers, leaves and the buds,
Young lovers – they meet with delight and mirth.

When virgin creepers expanding their arms,
Embrace the hearts of flourishing trees.
With a mild touch and bashful sight –
They murmur something to make them please.

And blooming flowers under Diana's grace,
Gaze at half – bloomed buds.
With open heart and craze –
They smile in response the matured buds.

I deeply feel your want or lack,
My darling nymph our days a back.

– (October' 1982)

## II

I ever remember your roseal lips,
Bloomed with odour when touched mine.
A sensation sweet I felt,
My breaths warm when touched thine.

I forget never your laughter sweet –
Those blooming Jasmine and rose together.
Even your whispers I precisely remember,
Sweet odour it spread you walked wherever.

Your frown or anger I noted per chance,
Enhance my fancy – my greatest pleasure.
I remember very well that catalyst,
For vapours of love – my life's treasure.

O' sombre night don't evoke the moan,
O' endless fancy now let my heart beat alone.

– (October' 1982)

## III

When virgin Diana with all her grace,
Lingers wrapped in light and shade.
Her crazy lover the cloud with a mild touch,
Kisses her darling, her new brocade.

Here on the earth mortal lovers unite together,
After long valediction.
They warmly greet, embrace each other,
With flowery hearts, imitate their action.

Flying creatures in their house naïve,
When warm each other in moonlight chill.
With fumes of love – their breaths,
Twitter perchance with satisfied will.

I deeply feel your want or lack,
My darling Beau our days a back.

– (October' 1982)

## IV

Ah! that rainbow of my arms,
Formed when creeped around your chest.
Caused of violet eyes, lips rose red,
And gown blue which adorned you best.

Then flowers bloomed, I forget not,
Yes, to watch that rainbow bright.
Crazy insects they appeared,
Like country lads to celebrate the sight.

Oh! when will it cease the frosty weather,
And appear again that rainbow bright.
I keenly wait – my nerves and veins,
To watch that sight.

O' Sombre time don't evoke the moan,
O' endless fancy now let my heart beat alone.

– (October' 1982)

# Two Beating Hearts In The Hope Of Union

## I

O' my dreaming heart, sweet seeking heart,
Calm breathing heart –
Slept in a beachen green,
Where blow the winds of carol.

And flowers bloom unfading,
Soaked within the nectar.
Where rejoice the crazy insects,
Finding great shelter on the whorls.

And if perchance cruel winds blow –
A curse to their calmity.
They tremble with fear,
And enhance their firmity.

Why sudden awake with thy rapid thrills,
Is the hour near when thy dream be fulfilled?

.

– (November' 1982)

## II

Rejoice, Rejoice my heart,
Blood, veins and nerves all.
Leave thy slumber long,
And listen the rapturous waves of Carol.

The hour is near when she and I,
I and she will meet further.
Where all my agony passes by,
In the midst of her murmur.

And we two, clasping our arms,
On the rainbow bright.
Singing love songs,
Will reach up to heaven's height.

Make haste O' time, O' sensation sweet,
My heart bewilders for a further meet.

– (November' 1982)

## III

O' the month of July and showers sweet,
A boon to poor creepers.
O' clouds of hope in the firmament,
I gaze thy path with half lived feature.

Oh, all alone in the world,
I tremble in the air.
With dry pale leaves,
Without gleam or glare.

Go, go, go forever from my life,
O' torture of June and welcome July.
Adieu O' sun, thy scorch thy bite,
Welcome O' showers thy pleasure high.

Lo and behold! My heart rejoices, be cheer,
Lament not, no fret no fever.

– (November' 1982)

## IV

Exult O' soul, why stand a gape!
Make haste and seek thy ornaments.
And flatter O limbs in premonition,
Like a happy peacock's plumes.

The hour is near when he and I,
'll embrace each other – shy!
Ah, thy touch I remember,
When all my fatigue of June passes by.

Then dressed with wings evergreen,
I'll flourish – a young nymph.
Under thy grace, thy showers of love,
Dance and sing the songs of triumph.

Make haste O' time, O' sensation sweet,
My heart bewilders for a further meet.

– (November' 1982)

# Two Beating Hearts After Long Valediction

## I

O' lady, sweet delicate nymph,
Of marked virtue of healing.
For my wounds caused by tortures,
Of way during Valediction!

I ever felt thy need,
In my veins.
With rapid flow of blood,
And load of affection!

Ever owed to thee,
Ever craved thy nectar.
When laid alone,
In the hour of dejection!

Lover mundane in the mundanity,
Seek thy shelter, I seeker of the beauty.

– (December' 1982)

## II

One impulse from thee,
And shower of nectar from thy lips.
Cause a great panic,
In my fatigue and futility of the earth.

One moment with you,
Thy blissful Union.
I enjoy the pleasure of heaven,
And forget all the weariness of the world.

Thy single glance, thy look,
I feel in my blood.
Like an ointment to my aching heart,
And plunge into abyss of the mirth.

O' beauty to the seeker of truth,
Thy whispers can utter whole of it.

– (December' 1982)

## III

Sun to the eve,
Moon to the morrow.
Ponds and pools,
To the ocean bid morrow.

Creepers grow,
And seek the banyans.
Flourishing buds,
To the flowers for Union.

And blows the air,
Through ether whole.
Why should I not,
A human soul.

Ever craved thy lusture, O' darling Beau,
Your shower of nectar for soul's hue.

– (December' 1982)

## IV

Ever bewilder'd ever perplex'd,
For thy sacred Union.
Reaches to calmity – my beating heart,
Like a river when mingles in the ocean.

Enjoys the supreme bliss,
Of great union.
When they carry the breezes,
On the path of breakers.

High and high,
More than Mount Everest.
Up to the peak of rapture,
Up to the height of heavens.

I seeker of calmity,
Reach at the peak of tranquility.

– (December' 1982)

## Fear And Frown In Love

Fear and Frown,
In the history of lovers.
Like a green – green beach,
Growing in the showers.

Fear resides ever,
In the minds of each.
Lest it dry,
The green – green beach.

But it dries never –
The beach of lovers.
Fear makes it soaked,
In the form of showers.

Anger or frown :- chase me not etc,
We often note.
Yes, a trick track of lovers,
For love to promote.

Frown acts,
Like a catalyst strong.
For the fumes of love,
And lovers song.

– (January' 1983)

## Blow, Blow O' Winds!

Blow, Blow O' winds,
From where my dear darling laid!
You can touch her soft red lips,
Bring a shower of nectar to my faded face.

A complete season has pass'd,
Since valediction.
What smile, what murmur sweet!
I precisely remember.

O' gentle breeze!
You may recognize her very ease.
Like a vernal wood,
Ever charming and please.

Moon her face stary sky brocade,
Like cloud of rain, her hair covers the face.
Creeper her limbs and the fingers,
Like you yourself she always lingers.

Make haste O' winds,
Embrace my body and soul too.
For I may feel,
Her laughter and whisper in you.

– (July' 1983)

## Love Never Dies

Season of flowers and fragrance,
Where cuckoo sings on the hue.
We cupid and the psyche, two loving bodies,
Were singing love songs sitting on the dew.

All of sudden,
A fear appears on the screen.
Mortal is the world and our mundane games,
Our love radiance, sight and scene.

Nay, Nay, Never, Love never dies,
Echoed the sound of our combined soul.
Love never dies and two loving souls,
Love will prevail is the truth whole.

Thus sitting on the grass in rapturous mood,
We cupid and psyche kissing each other echoed the wood.

– (October' 1983)

## I Hate You Sparrow

After day-long toil when the sun sets in the west,
Flowers, birds and animals all seek the rest.
Young lovers holding vases greet,
With heart beating fast – they meet.

What union of shrines – their soft red lips,
What flow of nectar where pilgrims take dips.
What breaths warm – sweet smelling incense,
What whispers sweet–ringing bells for cupid's presence.

Welcome cuckoo, sweet singing dryad,
Enhance our fancy in myriad.
What intoxication we feel, O' nymph of garden deep,
Clasping our arms we merge into sleep.

I hate you sparrow!
Morning bird cruel and narrow.
My lover bids adieu leaving me alone,
stop thy chirping, it evokes the moan.

– (October' 1983)

## Nectar Of Lovers

Water from the well, water from the valley,
From ponds, pools, rivers and streams all.
Fresh water is nectar,
Nectar for all.

Plants and animals, men and women,
Of all the ages.
Need water for life, freshwater to live,
In all the phases.

But water saline from two deep lakes,
Is nectar of lovers of all breed.
It preserves the love and lovers' lives,
Of all the culture, colour and creed.

Thus, we live, look fit and fine,
Playing love game – a game divine.

– (December' 1983)

# Meta-Physics

"Sing O' bird, thou teach me how to sing,
O' heaven, would that I had my wings."

"Sing O' lark, I'll teach you how to sing,
Come and soar with me, I have my wings."

# The Crossing

## I

Oh, many a moments have passed,
Hours, days and the years.
Season of clouds and the sky blue,
Stormy winds and gentle breeze as well.

Fruitful years of loaded crops,
With the echoes of nightingales.
And the years of barren fields,
Where sit the multitudes of owls.

Rivers and canals calm flowing,
Where rejoice the fish.
And wide desert with the sand burning,
Where run the deer in the mirage.

I exhale and inhale in the mundanity,
Between mirth and moan idea and reality.

– (January' 1988)

## II

It was delicate mourn,
Marked with the flowers blooming.
All white and red,
With their brims overflowing.

The air was calm–flowing,
And full of fragrance.
It seemed overjoyed the whole universe,
Bearing thy all-pervading essence.

And they twitter'd the morning bird,
A hymn to thee in thy praise.
Yes, to reveal thy presence,
They uttered the sacred phrase.

When I appeared bearing a blissful pipe,
Thou bestowed me sweeten my life.

– (January' 1988)

## III

Ever happy, ever feeling fresh,
I wandered in the forest wide.
Amid happy, happy lads – my playmates,
I blew my songs of pipe.

Several hills and valleys I cross'd,
Several fields of hawthorn.
But like velvet green I felt,
A delicate born.

And I often came to rest,
Under Bunyan tree.
Where fled in panic all fears,
When blew my pipe, I free.

Such was thy pipe thou bestowed me,
O' my father, I thank thee.

– (January' 1988)

## IV

I know not, I remember not,
Where I missed my pipe.
During my plays of childhood,
I lost my sweetest life.

Or someone thieved my songs,
During my sleep.
Come! Come! Come!
Make me aback, for ye I weep.

It comes not to me, my pipe,
Never 'll come again.
Few miles I walked thousands more,
Yes, a long long journey I have to gain.

Now how to walk and how to face the siege,
No one here to make me please.

– (January' 1988)

## V

A dark, dark forest,
Where grow the thorns.
I wandered a young lad,
I laughed, I mourned.

Thorns in the feet, thorns in the arms,
Thorns! Thorns! Thorns!
My bed on the hawthorn,
I bled! I bled! I bled!

O' my pipe, divine pipe,
Blow once again.
O' my father, O' my lord!
I crave thy presence – my sacred aim.

Thus I sat and mourned,
My face withered and cloths torn.

– (January' 1988)

## VI

Many a man have pass'd,
Here threw they not a single glance.
Some said tut and moved in disgust,
Their eyes had no further chance.

All drunkards, they thought me drunkard,
Poor themselves, declared me a beggar.
Fools! Why should I beg?
I seek my biggest treasure.

I closed my eyes,
A flow of tears, yes to lessen my bother.
Ah! someone soothed my limbs,
Perhaps, my father.

My heart rejoiced, I gazed around,
But none was there, few pearls on the ground.

– (January' 1988)

## VII

Clouds, dark dark clouds,
Heavy hails and the cyclones.
O' World! O' Life! O' Journey!
Tortures in plural and I alone.

I fell unconscious on the bed of thorns,
And covered me all dry pale leaves.
Oh! the oozes of blood,
From my body – The Sieve.

And when I woke, I amazed –
Petals white and red!
Where they vanished my wounds,
And tyranny of the bed.

Ah! My father, a little peace I feel,
This young nymph's face my wounds to heal.

– (January' 1988)

## VIII

A little peace, a moment's shelter,
But I have to' seek the eternal peace.
Endless source of nectar not rainy fountain,
Evergreen shelter, not the shadow of deciduous trees.

Soothe me not O' World!
By giving me frail baby toys.
Hinder not my way O' mortal fruits,
I seek the eternal Joys.

Make not me captive O' golden cage!
Weaken not my plumes.
Let me soar and soar high,
Where unfading flowers bloom.

Don't stand agape my soul, proceed further,
Miles to go to reach thy father.

– (February' 1988)

## IX

Tempters! Tempt me not,
Go aside, lead me not.
O' haughty tempters shake me not,
O' satanic creatures char me not.

Go! Go! Go!
Deprive me not from my father.
Wake! Wake! O' deity wake!
Save me, my soul from acute bother.

Oh overpowered, overpowered am I,
I am overpowered by the beasts.
Lo and behold the countless hosts!
Call me at banquet, call me at feasts.

No, no, never, I don't take the wordily wine,
O' the blood of fox, wolf and swine.

– (February' 1988)

## X

How to win? How to live? How to reach?
When I have lost my pipe.
Miles to go, now miles to go,
When I have lost my treasure of life.

How to cross the ocean,
When I have lost my pipe thou gave to me.
They leave me not the leeches,
I bleed in the abyss of the sea.

They deck my body the dirty scales,
And it comes to me the shark.
Pull me above the soaring bird,
Sweet singing bird – The Lark.

Sing O' bird, thou teach me how to sing,
O' heaven! Would that I had my wings.

– (February' 1988)

## XI

Hark! Hark! O' my soul!
Who knocked at thy door.
The door is shut,
Unbar the door.

Bar the door, bar the door,
Storm is violent tonight.
And they wonder the cruel beasts,
Too bold to fight.

Now check me not, prevent me not,
Tonight 'll be bright.
Either they win,
Or never 'll challenge my might.

What use to live under their sinful throne,
Like a dumb, like a mute, in utter groan.

– (February' 1988)

## XII

I unbar the door,
But what, no beast, no storm was there!
Ah! a bright radiance dazzled my room,
Sterile and bare.

O' thou have come my lord!
Come! Come! Come!
In my meanest hut of hay,
Thou are welcome!

Make haste O' soul, don't stand agape,
Thy father has come to thy place.
Bring what you have in the honour of lord,
Thy father has come to thy place.

Tears! Tears! Tears! A flood of tears,
Oh, nothing except the necklace of tears.

– (February' 1988)

## XIII

Rest! Rest! Rest my father!
Abode is thine, thou ever rest.
My poetic heart thy temple,
Flowers of worship – the verse.

Both 'PRANA' and 'APANA',
Grant them sweet smelling incense,
And my utterance to thee,
Tolling bells for thy presence.

Make my life pure, O' the purest!
Make my path bright, O' the brightest!
Forgive my sins, forgiveness thy virtue,
Lead my way, O' the best knower of Truth.

Here is the soul, I care not thou care it,
O' the wittiest soul, I have no wit.

– (February' 1988)

## XIV

The storm is over, the fight is over,
Yes, the fight is over forever.
Adieu! O' haughty tempters,
O' cruel beasts, you never.

O' leeches, the shark and the hammer!
To all I bid adieu.
Tut, O' dirty scales and shell slippery,
Now I'm dressed with the wings new.

And O' the thorns and the bed of hawthorns,
Now tortures not my life.
O' dry pale leaves deck me not,
I have regained my pipe.

Sing O' lark, I'll teach you how to sing,
Come and soar with me, I have my wings.

– (March' 1988)

## XV

The black thick curtain,
Has vanished now.
How emits the radiance,
And glitters how!

His glory peeps from the sun,
And odour from the blooming flowers.
How he gesticulates,
In children's sweet shower.

Lo and behold! his countless arms,
To embrace thee, embrace them.
Hark the sacred words of thy father,
To guide thy path, follow them.

Now the way is clear and full of pleasure,
Light divine to seek thy treasure.

– (March' 1988)

## XVI

Here flourish the garden in my soul,
Where unfading flowers bloom.
Intoxicated am I with odour divine,
Where comes not gloom?

And it sings the cuckoo – the sacred hymn,
To enhance my pleasure.
When I rest,
In my sleep or hours of leisure.

The winds are lovely,
They flow in calmness.
Slowly, Slowly touch my heart,
To remind thy greatness.

Thus I travel by night and day,
No darkness deep, no torture of the way.

– (March' 1988)

## XVII

And parting kiss to you all,
Now I must depart.
See, see in the firmament,
With arms expanding he smiles – the smart.

Who pulls me up,
Forever, Forever!
Rejoice O' brothers, lament not,
Never, Never!

The sun is shining in the horizon,
And the winds favourable to cross the bar.
Listen to the breakers and the winds,
They spread the Carol.

Ah, holding vases he greets,
O' world, O' journey to my father I meet.

– (March' 1988)

# Misery of a Pond

Hark! Hark! O' my Idler soul,
Don't stand agape.
My heart pains,
Yes, someone's misery takes the shape.

Whence and whose words,
Of groan I hear.
The voice comes from the pond,
They utter the waves very dear.

"Calm and clam,
Where bloom the flowers,
You think of me,
I know.

Ever tranquill I rest,
Where rejoice the fish.
You think of me,
I know.

True to think O visitor!
But why I groan!
Why lament,
Do you know?

Behold!
They come the wilders –
A curse to calmness,
A curse to my tranquility.

No flowers will spread the nectar now,
No fish rejoice.
And 'll perish the Carol,
To hear their loud noise.

Cruel beasts – they come and go,
And I rejoice and mourn.
Ever seek the bliss,
I ocean born."

– (April' 1988)

## Pleasure Of An Idler

Who is he,
Sitting still a human kind.
Gazes towards the Pleiades,
With tranquill mind?

Towards the grass,
And smiles now.
Slowly, slowly he walks,
Parleying with himself how?

"Idler, he is an idler"
I heard from the crowd,
"Half mad is he,
Weaving his shroud."

No, not half mad,
I protest, O' gentlemen!
An absolute mad is he,
Far from the crowd of half – mad men.

A mad far from,
The fret and fever of the earth,
What he seeks in the silence
Do you know?

From leaf to leaf,
His eyes move in interrogation.
What he wants to determine,
Do you know?

Every impulse of the nature,
Takes harmony with his heart.
And he reaches to the place unique,
The idler smart.

And he laughs and forgets himself,
In utter delight.
An absolute mad,
In divine light.

This is all, all about a mad,
You do not know.
Yes, pleasure of a Idler,
You do not know.

– (April' 1988)

## I Fear, Lest I Become A Millionaire

Then I'll pass my days,
Among the crowd of men,
Men of my own status –
The Elite.

And the servants,
Of the royal palace,
As swift as air,
'll wait for my orders.

Clubs –
Wit, wine and women,
And meetings arranged,
Meetings without adjourn.

I'll precede them,
They greet.
Hark! Echoes of slogans –
Live long the royal seat.

But what,
This wooden chair!
O' my fancy had brought me,
Up to the heights of the Mayor!

Adieu, O' fruitless ambition!
For I fear, lest I become a millionare.
And forget my pleasure,
Pleasure of an Idler.

To sit still on the grass and contemplate,
Amid happy, happy flowers,
Where spreads the nightingale,
Her melodious shower.

Goddess of riches – O' Laxmi!
I dishonor you not.
But true, thy glorious burden,
I cannot.

Come, come to my life,
You ever come.
But slowly, slowly,
You are welcome.

For I may breathe,
Without suffocation.
Suffocation that an idler feels,
When captured in the golden prison.

– (May' 1988)

## The Cloud

Wait, Wait O' winds!
My feet deny.
This void vast,
And tortures many.

I soar and soar,
Far from the base – my master or mate.
Slowly blow, my heart breaks to pieces,
O' cruel, cruel fate.

It was a place very calm and quite,
I remember.
Where dwells the peace of every kind,
Who made me asunder?

That supreme bliss –
Thy sacred union, I enjoyed.
Where cometh not even the shadow of grief,
I felt overjoyed.

Now, why I here,
To bear the whips of fate?
It is dashed my body,
And I bleed.

But ah! who smiles here?
It seems a delicate nymph.
Tut, O' misfortune, your hour is gone,
And Lo, here is the triumph!

She walks in beauty,
My limbs flourish.
Slowly, slowly, O' my heart!
The flood is great, lest you perish.

Thanks O' heaven, O' father!
Your grace.
It heals my wounds,
This young nymph's face.

I name ye 'Diana',
Yes, my love, my lips utter.
Ah! come in closer darling,
It craves my heart thy nectar.

Let me embrace thy breast,
Coy not, O' dove!
Thy heart beats too, they show,
Thy cheeks full marks of love.

I was bleeding an hour before,
And it dashed my heart.
Is it thy touch, thy embrace?
All my fatigue is gone, I am smart.
This flowery bath we'll walk together,
Clasping arms forever, forever.
Though the winds are cruel and strong too,
But lovers win ever.

Hark! Hark! O' Diana,
Who utters my name?
The voice comes from the earth,
Yes, it muddles our game.

Ah! your looks are lovely,
And pleasant too.
But leave me my darling,
I have to keep my promise too.

Leave me not my heart pains,
I tremble. I fear,
What you said an hour before,
'Clasping arms forever, forever!'

Thy grief, thy moan, thy tears,
All weaken me.
Think a little of love –
Immortal! it's never to die.

But glory is once gone,
It cometh never.
Last kiss my darling, till we meet further,
Yes, forever, forever.

– (July' 1988)

## On A Rainy Evening

After seasons burning like a furnace,
Appear dense clouds in the sky.
Poor farmers, peacocks and the souls of poets,
With open Joys do spring high.

Like elephants mad they wander the clouds,
And trembles the ocean to hear their voice loud.
My heart joys with the mirth of withered soil,
That craves the nectar after long summer's toil.

Lo, listen the tip – tap of nectar drops.
Awaking and soothing the faded grass.
Behold, these minute seeds opening their slumber long.
With the sun and sweet music of birds' song.

See, see! the grass, the plants and the trees,
Dancing like maids overjoyed and please,
These jumping frogs and lower creatures,
Chanting the God – his glory and feature.

What cattle grazing! What bleating lambs!
What sounding drums and dancing lads!
What farmers ploughing! What maiden's song!
What rainbow bright in the void long!

O', ye nectar drop whence you come?
Why you come? And where you mingle again.
Yes, from the infinite sea, giving life to the lifeless being,
You mingle again.

O' the showers of nectar you flow from ponds and pools,
To the rivers and streams to the sea infinite.
Take me with you, I'm tired of life,
I lament, I weep for the eternal light.

But Hark! A murmur dear,
Perhaps my conscience voice.
Lo, it is very clear,
Listen, Listen it twice.

Man's life is but like a drop of water,
Giving its nectar to the faded beings.
Changing dross into dancing hue,
With mirth and delight merges into the blue.

You have to awake the sleeping seeds,
Your love and affection to faded beings.
Before you mingle into ocean deep,
Before you mingle into ocean deep.

– (July' 1988)

## To The Storm

Season of clouds and storm,
Full of sound of thunderbolts.
Bright light pierces the heart of sky,
Whole nature doth seem making deep sigh.

They lose their path the flying creatures,
And run in the panic the wild features.
How wavers the heart of the ocean cold,
To hear the sound of thunderbolts.

Leaves, flowers and fruits become offering to the nature,
And half - bloomed buds 'll never come to feature.
Giant trees all - over around,
Are falling on the ground with heavy sound.

Now I prefer to sit amidst nature,
To enjoy, To know and To think its feature.
Deep sounding clouds enhance my tranquility,
It's shining and splendour illuminate my faculty.

I see none, nowhere around me,
Except myself and thee.
I, a spirit, leaving my body alone,
Fly hither and thither to hear thy tone.

What I see a numberless troops,
Of fallen leaves, buds and fruits.
Leaving the world to the blissful seat,
With joy, with mirth to their father they meet.

O' the storm full of light,
O' leaves, O' buds and fruits on the flight.
Take me with you, I'm tired of life,
I want to see the eternal light.

Now, O' ye cloud! my goal, thy goal,
Lift me up, my bleeding soul.
My heart bewilders and veins too,
To reach my father, my home true.

– (September' 1988)

# To The Eternity

I lay in grief in a solitude,
On the bank of Ganga with weary attitude.
I was alone to shed the tear,
Tears of worldly fret and fever.

The flow of river was calm and quiet,
Amid two broad lines of sand white.
It was gloomy as I observed,
No joy, no zeal for life it observed.

Once upon a time during the flowers,
I saw it's sweet and mirthful hours.
It was then in its golden age,
Symbol of youth – The best phase.

Season of clouds and thunder I remember,
I forget not it's horrible temper.
Roaring loud, running very fast,
Uprooting the trees gigantic and vast.

Thus it shows it's various phases,
Never forgets its flow passing through ages.
Eternal flow its duty its fame,
To merge into ocean its wise aim.

Leap, leap my heart lament not more,
What is life? To flow evermore.
In pleasure or pain bearing the aim,
To merge into God, your origin, your claim.

– (November' 1988)

## To The Sovereign

Who is he that controls the sunset and its dawn,
Enforces the flowers to bloom on the lawn.
And regulates the change of seasons on the ground,
Tides in ocean and winds around.

Who is he that gives red colour and smell to rose,
What fragrance it has, why not dog rose?
Plants get food by growing roots deeper,
But how is nurtured the immortal creeper?

We see the lotus, it blooms during day,
But white lily under moon gay.
The rainbow appears during the rain,
Fresh fruits of plum in winter alone.

My heart leaps with mirth and delight,
Whole earth is dressed with divine light.
Every pulse of the nature chants thy name,
Unending glory and eternal fame.

O' God, O' God! everywhere is visible thy great presence,
Yet they seek the null existence.
Dispel our darkness and dense defect,
Our sorrow, our misery and wrong concept.

You made the nature duty bound,
Why not men apart on the ground.
Fill our minds with the sense of duty,
Source of delight and natural beauty.

– (November' 1988)

## To The Solitudes

Those sanguine colour'd cliffs of mountains,
Chirping birds and sound of fountains.
The moon, the Star and the sky blue,
Cool, cool breezes and permanent hue.

I remember, I feel in my veins,
And forget all my tortures and pains.
Then soar and soar up to the height of heaven,
Far from the madding crowd of men.

What pretty squirrel with a piece of nut,
Made her way towards it's nest.
And winked her younger ones to come together,
To share the pieces among all the brothers.

What running stream without a leisure,
To flow evermore, thy best pleasure.
Thy murmur sweet utter thy soul,
No rest, No sleep before reaching the goal.

And there in the heaven walks the moon,
Her crazy lover follows her soon.
They embrace each other and whisper too,
Immortal is the love and lovers too.

O' bless'd teacher, the greatest teacher!

Consoling friend, and moral teacher.

A moment with you, I feel in paradise,

No tortures, no pains of the world – wide.

– (December' 1988)

## Adam's Letter To The God

O' God, O' Father, O' Lord!
Why I here in the place unique?
It is very fearsome and full of thorns,
Those were paths full of flowers, here I bleed.

Are you angry father? For what?
That I've eaten the fruit of forbidden tree.
Yes, I disobeyed, realize my sin,
And strive my best to be free.

Here I lament by night and day,
Your grace, Eve is sharing my tortures of the way.
It is some sort of Peregrination,
You'll call after short duration.

But the way is dark and intricate,
Lest I forgot my way.
These number less tunnels dark and deep,
For a beam of light, I weep, I weep.

When I rest after day long toil,
I think of you and that blessed soil.
Then tears flow for your realization,
Don't you hear my lamentation.

Call me father, call me forever,
Forget my sin, I never.
I'm thy child, thy ignorant child,
Your own son, sweet and mild.

Nay, let me struggle for redemption,
I beg nothing except thy attention.
The earth is lovely though dark and deep,
Full of thorns but flowers to spread.

Rest is well, my dear divine,
You are welcome abode is thine.
I wish to see thee, my heart springs high,
I'll wait, till I die, I'll wait till I die.

– (December' 1988)

# When I Sit Alone

Who pulls me here towards solitude,
God's grace, my heart is full of gratitude.
What a place it is! Calm and quiet,
Full of beautiful scenes and sights.

Moon in the heaven with treasure nectareous,
Adored by stars like flowers gregarious.
And on the grass, where bloom the hawthorns,
Embrace my heart the nature's arms.

Adieu! O' flood of the madding crowd,
Where people weave and weave their shrouds.
Utter peace I feel amidst green, green mutes,
Where creepers dance to the music of flutes.

O' Goddess of solitude, O' fair nymph!
Moments with you – my victory my triumph.
Lo, tears flow, O' deity in thy esteem,
My soul glitters now I awake or dream.

Now I can see the whole universe,
And can listen its unified verse.
The verse divine I can feel in my veins,
When showers the peace and perish my pains.

Rest, Rest, Rest, O' My heart,
In nature's shrine.
I'll be thy priest O' green, green hue,
Let them run behind the blood-red wine.

Dream, Delight and Dew drops,
Are mine.
Let them run behind the blood –
Blood of Fox, Wolf and Swine.

– (December 1988)

# The Labyrinth

A solitude, what an abode of peace!
Far from the noise of the crowd.
Where laid a hermitage,
Made of wild grass and wood.

At the entrance of it sat a saint picturesque,
Bearded, Calm breathing and statuesque.
Sandel - pasted forehead and face red,
What a holy person! I bowed my head.

A year passed or two,
I had a further chance to you.
But what a change, I wonder!
No grass, no wood but a fine home was yonder.

Built for protection, I thought,
From hail and storm, cold and hot.
I thanked God and returned,
And decided once more to take my turn.

A year passed or two,
I had a further chance to you.
But what a change, never seen in life,
A cow, A dog, A wench - his wife!

This may be what! nothing else,
Other than the world – labyrinth.
We boats – men try to escape from thee,
Alas! we fall and fall into thee.

Need not to escape, not to worry,
Learn how to walk on the breakers, make hurry.
The world is like a lab – divine,
Where you can search the source of shine.

– (December' 1988)

## Tear'd Mutes

"Eternal silence!
Silence under shivering stars.
Yes, hunger by licking,
And cold by sticking.

This is all –
Our fate – our happiness.
Happiness of rural workers,
Pleasure of the peasant."

## An Embryonic Dream

A Pregnant hen laid an egg,
Snow white bright and big.
She nurtur'd it with love and care,
For she had dreamt of chicken fair.

Day and night she sat on it,
In order to protect from cold and hit.
She had a dream – a beautiful dream,
Of a new hatched chicken as soft as cream.

She would shut her eyes perchance,
To feel within a beautiful glance.
A beautiful hatch around her wings,
In the open air twitters and sings.

And embryo too was thinking of the earth,
A place very unique – of delight and mirth.
Under shell of lime he felt unease,
And tried to escape from it at ease.

He had an image of previous pleasures,
And ever remembered these precious treasures.
His view of life was never pessimistic,
He hanker'd for the eath, he was optimistic.

Life under the sun he precisely remember'd,
Spring flowers and grains of December.
Meadows, green fields and the mountains,
Ponds, pools and the fountains.

But I's desires seldom fulfill,
Too weak against the world's will.
What happen'd a day, cruel devil came,
Boiled the egg and finished the game.

Poor hen was crying against human deed,
Man has nothing, an embryo to feed!
Oh, it has gone my beautiful dream,
My lovely hatch as soft as cream.

Think a little, O' men, think of your brothers' cry,
An embryo is not a thing to fry.
Till soil is fertile and full of hue,
Yes, soil is fertile and full of hue.

– (February' 1988)

## I Weep For You, O' Poor Creatures!

O' poor creatures on the earth,
From the heights of air to the abyss deep.
Give thy ears to me,
O mutes, for ye I weep!

Say, what you utter,
By night and day in a secret tone.
Make it clear to me – your voice,
For I may assert your mirth and moan.

O' airy creatures, you soar,
More rapid than my Imagination!
Wait, wait O' darling for a moment,
For I may catch thy fickle attention.

O' fish of pretty colour and size,
What fickleness thou possess, I wonder,
My caprice fails, it follows you not,
Be yonder!

And you innocent land dwellers,
Poor, Poor creatures!
Amid terrible world of human,
Appears your half – lived feature.

Hark! Hark!
What I listen! Perhaps their voice.
They utter the breakers,
And winds of all sides, Lo, listen it twice!

See, see, O' human!
Their rapid motion and listen their songs too.
Look, when they gaze or leap on a streap,
Their innocent looks and bleats too.

But a single glance, yes a single glance,
Don't forget to throw on butchers' shops –
Which'll reveal their voice clear,
Their dirgeful cry, moan and the fear.

Behold that crowd,
A long, long queue!
Their hunger for blood,
They hate the hue.

O' cruel human beings!
Be cheer and strong.
But forget not, yes, slaughter not,
Your own brothers' song.

– (January' 1990)

## Insecta

Insecta –
O' the insects of the Universe!
Assemble together,
I crave thy music to support my verse.

Most dirty, most ugly,
Most hateful creatures –
They say the human,
Do you know?

Nay, your short lives,
Your half – lived life.
Your gloomy feature,
Do you know?

Nay, bearing a half – lived life,
You try to yourself hide.
But their envy,
They made the insecticide!

Ye lament not poor creatures,
You have your glory too!
Your mimic divine and murmur sweet,
Spread on the earth your music true!

– (July' 1990)

## Wounded Dove – The Woman

Why on the earth, O' Eve!
To bear the whips of Adam.
To shed tears,
And breathe in suffocation?

No cuckoo sings in the Eden,
No flowers bloom yet.
Spring awaits thee,
And the air wanders in interrogation.

And here on the dirt,
Under dusky moon.
Thy shies vanish in the winds,
You bleed.

O' wretched Adam,
Wake!
Thy eyes seem,
As if the devil still tempts thee.

See, thy Eve –
Thy father made her to thee.
Near thy heart to love,
Yes, only to love.

But, alas!

Like a tear'd dove.

Wounded by hawk,

She breathes her last.

– (July' 1990)

## A Child And The Crust

A beggar child in the search of Crust,
Wanders here and there.
And even at the mud,
His vessel remains empty and bare.

“A burden to the nation,
Cancer of the Country”
He hear’d around,
But not a single word of sympathy.

Well he pass’d the crowd,
By and By.
That poor child of seven perhaps,
With tears in the eyes.

And amid the big slum now,
In a dark, dark room.
That figure vanished,
Into the doom.

Where lay a drunkard devil –
The Satan.
To devour the sweet existence,
Of Adam.

Thus deprived of his mother's breasts,
He lived and partly lived.
That child alone in the world,
With his father – The Devil.

Never kiss'd his mouth,
Anyone.
Nor did sing a lullable,
To make him sleep.

The child could not sleep,
That night too.
Nor could he weep,
Or whisper a word of complain.

But the hunger –
The abdomen's fire.
Compelled him,
To retire.

And his little feet now,
Went towards the goal.
Where he could find a little crust,
To soothe his soul.

Lo, and behold! A fungus coated bread,
On a heap of rubbish.
His eyes glitter'd and cried he,
Ureka! Ureka! in the fit of rapture.
But none could hear his voice of triumph,
Except a tear'd dog.
Who carried the bread there,
The true instrument of God.

– (July' 1990)

## The Golden Cage And The Bird

From the grassy plains to the Everest,
Under the bright sun of march.
Doth spread the sweetest music,
Of the mild monarch.

What virgin buds for a glance of flowers!
Full of craze they dance in the showers.
What creepers cry in the fit of Union!
Slowly walk towards the Banyans.

What rivers of snow full of pride!
Reach to the calmity when mingle in the wide.
What flighty nymphs on the hills and valleys!
Dwarfs on the fields and dryads on the trees.

But brake, what aching sound,
From the golden cage, ye hark?
It seems like a dirge,
Perhaps sings a lark.

"Season of flowers and fragrance,
And the clear blue sky.
I often soared in the air,
Near the heavens high.

The twitter of my friend,
In the hour of rapture.
But like a dream now,
I remember.

Spring comes and goes still,
And flowers bloom yet.
But, I the poorest behind the golden cage,
Shed the tear like Lady of Shallot."

Heaven is lovely,
And the air.
But a cry in vain,
O' the prisoner of the Mayor.

Rest, Rest, Rest O' bird!
In a corner of the cage.
But forget not, yes, forget not to sing,
Thy right against the human rage.

– (December' 1990)

# Dear Son Of God

Who is he coming on the way?
Slowly, Slowly, not happy nor gay.
Lean and thin like a ghost or spectre,
No shine in the eyes nor zeal in the picture.

His face wrinkled, no cloth in the upper half,
To cover, is essential, the lower half.
A wrinkled basket his infinite treasure –
His fate, his happiness and the treasure.

No slogan he knows except 'one penny sir',
His religion,
His duty,
His right, contemplation and murmur!

Who is his companion? None,
No one except a stick bent.
His parents, his children,
His wife, teacher and the friend.

He knows no Quilt or Cushion,
Nor season change.
Earth and sky, earth and sky,
In the winter, rain or temperature high.

O' God! O' God! Same soul, same body,
Same blood, bone and breath.
One in the dust, one in the palace high,
One down – trodden, one elite, but why?

O' Dear, Dear Son of God,
Come, Come my brother in your period odd.
When among the crowd your whispers lost,
Like a drop in the desert, like a drop in the hearth.

– (May' 1992)

# A Wounded Dog

It was 'KABRA' – A creature black and white,
I often saw in the street of my house.
To him everyone was his lord,
And he himself was the guard.

He filled his stomach poor creature pale,
With the pieces of bread waste and stale.
Then he barked by night and day,
When saw a stranger on that way.

Thus he lived and partly lived,
Between hunger and satiety.
And greed and contentment,
On mercy of the people their lived.

It so happened a day a stranger came,
To crush his half – lived life,
To crush his pale existence,
He fought boldly but lost the game.

Now developed deep wounds on his shoulder,
Due to sudden attack of a dog bolder.
Who made him deprive of his share stale,
And crushed his glory and turned the tale.

When bad luck comes it never alone,
Those who were his masters,
Were changed and now no more masters,
Fie! Pooh! Tut! such were their tones.

At last he died a dog death,
With tears in his eyes,
On wounds flies,
He died poor dog, a dog death.

How selfish we are great homo sapien,
A poor dog died, a faithful being.
Because of hunger, because of wound,
Because of hunger, because of wound.

– (May' 1992)

## Under Shivering Stars

(Pleasure of the Peasant)

"What's here for the stomach,
For abdomen's fire,
To breathe to lament,
And to suffer?"

"Dross and dirt,
Mixed with the salt of eyes.
Here is it,
To enhance our sighs. "

(They dine and lie on the hay
under shivering stars)

"Is it our reward,
Of day long toil?
Is it our fate,
fate of the workers on the soil? "

" Me often think of delicious dishes,
Palace royal and the Cushions.
Me often think to dress myself,
And thee, my dear, dear beloved.

But nay, A dream in vain,
For we are born to be silent,
And shed tears,
Tears in the honour of goddess melancholy.
Eternal silence!
Silence under shivering stars.
Yes, hunger by licking,
And cold by sticking.

This is all –
Our fate, our happiness.
Happiness of rural workers,
Pleasure of the peasant."

(A flood of tears
in their deep, deep eyes.)

"Sleep is miles away,
From the eyes."
"Yes, sleep is miles away,
From the eyes."

"Come in close my darling,
Till the sun appears in the east,
For I may forget all my toil,
Within thy breasts."

(They embrace each other

their outer and the inner.)

– (December' 1992)

## How Falls The Night In A Countryside

How falls the night in a Countryside,
Do you know?
How peeps the moon into the huts,
Do you know?

How calves bleat,
And cats mew?
How flutter the leaves,
And falls the dew?

How hoot the owls,
And nightingale sings?
How winds rustle,
And bats flap wings?

And how weeps the baby,
For his mother's breast?
When she cooks the rice,
For evening feast?

Then how they sleep,
On the bed of hay?
With teary eyes,
Yet happy and gay!

– (December' 1992)

## A Pair Of Dove

I often saw two lovely creatures,
Innocent born.
Far from the human crowd,
During my walks of the morn.

A pair of doves in a vernal wood,
Where dwells the peace.
Far from the fret and fever of the world,
On a banyan tree.

Where cometh not,
The shadow of gloom.
Ever soaked with nectar,
Fresh flowers bloom.

Never blows the air,
Of selfish motive.
Nor winds of Jeal,
Among woodland natives.

There they lived,
Two innate mutes.
But full of music,
To strike my lute.

Ever owed to them,
In my hours of leisure.
Ever thought of them,
In my hours of pleasure.

But in a morn what I see,
In the weather of hail.
Tear'd dove alone was only there,
To say and sing his tragic tail.

"What happened a day,
She and I close together.
Soared and soared,
In the mild warm weather.

From branch to branch,
Of flower'd trees.
We two were happy,
In gentle breeze.

Where flutter'd the flies,
Over flourishing buds.
Bearing the nectar,
Of matured ones.

Our feathers flourished,
In the fit of rapture.
We gazed in silence,
Each other's feature.
Our feathers flourished,
In the fit of rapture.
We gazed in silence,
Each other's feature.

At the moment there,
Came a man your brother.
And shot a fire,
He, seeker of the pleasure!

She fainted and fell,
My darling dear.
I made a cry,
With misery and fear.

Thus did ruin that man,
My whole treasure –
A prey to thy brother,
A prey to his pleasure!

But still remains,

A flood of tears in my eyes.

Which'll reveal our hearts,

To men wise!"

– (May' 1994)

## An Old Woman – Cow Dung Collector

I remember that summer evening,
When passing through a solitude.
I saw an old woman sitting among,
Cows and cow lads in multitude.

It was getting dark,
The sun had settled in the west.
Flock of the birds on the top of trees,
With a noise of chirp seeking their nest.

Now sudden silence,
Silence under the moon.
But that woman on the field,
Was still collecting cow dung – her boon.

Here on the dirt,
She was alone.
None was there,
To hear her moan.

Wrapp'd in a dirty sheet of cotton,
She gazed at me.
That woman alone in the world,
I knew.

I saw her face,
Wrinkled and pale.
Tears in the eyes,
Were telling her tale.

Never touched her heart,
The wings of golden bird.
For a piece of cloth, for a piece of bread,
She was breathing alone in the world.

That evening too,
She did collect a heap of dry cow dung.
And something sweet in that silence,
Did utter her tongue.

She wanted me,
To put her basket on her head.
"Angel of God", whisper her lips,
And she walked towards her shade.

I felt her tears,
Drops of tear on my arm.
Tears of a woman,
Wet and warm.

– (May' 1994)

# O' Shelley, Thy Lark Is Breathing Its Last

It was Tuesday,
Market day in the village.
People were busy in buying,
And selling the things.

Things were there,
All big and small.
Fruits, flowers,
And vegetable all.

I was there,
An idler unique.
To visit the market,
According to my freak.

Slowly I walked,
To the distal end.
Full of sun,
And cool wind.

My eyes moved,
All around.
Surprised to see the scene,
On the ground.

Big bamboo baskets full of,
Birds very fine.
Of varying size,
And colour divine.

Hens, Sparrows and pigeons,
Marked with patches Light and dark.
And Lo and behold,
Sweet singing Lark.

Twelve in numbers,
Their little feet tied.
They flutter'd their wings,
To be free and fly.

All they gazed towards the sky,
The sun and the cloud.
All play mates while they soar'd,
Now helpless to hear their chirp aloud.

They gazed towards me,
With tears in the eyes.
But a visitor I was,
Like all men wise.

Lo, and behold!
Appeared a hag meanwhile.
A woman of fifty,
Cruel, Wretched and Vile.
She glared the larks,
And danced around.
How much it costs,
She made the sound.

'Three hundred and fifty,
Take them all.'
Uttered the man,
'Delicious and healthy in a cost small.'

Thus they were sold,
Sweet singing Lark.
In the hands of a hag,
Wicked human hawk.

She put them all,
Into a bag small.
No cloud, no sun,
No air at all.

Thus they lost their melody,
In that utter dark.
None was there,
On the earth to hark.

Hark, O' cruel men!
O' homosapiens.
Twittering birds, sweet singing birds,
Are not to eat, O homosapiens!

– (May' 1994)

# Miscellaneous

"Oh, my heart perils,
And the innocent pen,
Save me.

And let my life be,
Constant, calm and tranquill,
Like thee."

"Save Melpomene,
O' Goddess of Tragic arena.
Save the earth from BRUTAS vile,
Save the human endangered while."

## On Playing Badminton

Shot! I was ready,
To defend myself.
And just placed it.
Calamity would have,
Fallen to me,
Had I not used my wit.

Thus a happy man,
I was there,
To face further.
O' Tricky Temptor,
Left, Right, Short and Long,
To make me bother.

But Nay, O' lad,
Too weak to make,
My racket bereaved.
Till I have,
My paces awake,
And limbs not tired.

– (December' 1987)

## To The Sky

Why agape?
I gaze towards the sky,
Infinite, immortal, awake and still.
What music thee possess!
I soar and soar
In the world azure, O' tranquill.

Let me utter my words,
And give thy ears to me,
I wonder.
O' ascetic to thee,
My Joys and sorrows,
I wish to surrender.

Lo and behold!
The source of nectar – my love, the nymph,
To make my love immortal.
What murmur! What whisper!
What shower in the silence!
I awake or sleep, I wonder.

And here, behold!
Who ran? A boy of seven perhaps,
And cried.
Eureka! Eureka!
For what? On a heap of rubbish, he finds.
A fungus-coated bread.
See more, a single glance here too –
A leprous
Wounded and teary.
None, no one bold,
Yes, not a single here,
To embrace the weary.

Oh! my heart perils,
And the innocent pen,
Save me.
And let my life be,
Constant, calm and
Tranquill like thee.

– (January' 1988)

## On Melancholy

Alas! I have nothing,
I see the happy faces of people.
But not a silver smile on my face,
Others are plundering the treasure, I only dream.

See! he is the favourite of goddess Laxmi,
Behold! he is the cupid enjoying nymphs.
These are clubs full of wit, wine and women,
And Lo! and behold these fortune's favourite – The Elite.

Let them enjoy. Mine be the melancholy,
Adieu! wealth, power and honour, mine be the contentment.
Let them run behind the shadows, mne be the base,
Farewell endless ambitions, mine be the eternal peace.

Where dwells the peace?
Neither on the earth, nor on the heavens.
You need a character, character without stain,
You need a base, other than mirage.

Welcome melancholy – mother to the eternal peace,

Embrace my body and soul too.

Come, come melancholy, ever come in my life,

I shall be thy priest, O' Goddess melancholy.

– (February' 1988)

## Verse, O' Verse!

"What'll please you, O' man!
In the hours of seclusion,
When bid you adieu,
This world of illusion.

Yes, cold death'll devour,
All else a day.
Futile is the vessel,
And toys of the play."

"Ay, what you utter, O' Stranger!
Stop, say no more.
Yes, I've my verse, verse, O' verse,
To verse, I adore.

Where is my flute –
A talent worth laud,
My father bestowed me,
When sent abroad.

Now let me sing,
The song of Joys,
Song immortal,
Of mortal toys!

Which'll echo,

In the heaves bare.

To please my soul,

Forever forever."

– (March' 1988)

## The Oasis

Lo, here's an oasis,
The green, green hue.
Welcome joys,
And pains all adieu.

O' sandy winds,
The scorching sun and the sight!
Rush in the mirage,
I bid adieu.

Now sing O' bird,
Thy songs of infinite joy.
With some of mine,
To make my alloy.

And O' dear Coco,
Palm and the cactus green.
With arms expanded you all,
Come, ever come to my mental screen.

When my arid heart,
Needs thy affection.
And lips utter thee,
In the hours of dejection.

Or when drop-down unconscious,

In my journey of miles myriad.

Crave a shower of nectar,

I, sufferer, O' Dryad!

– (April' 1988)

## To The Poetic Muse

O' poetic muse, ye knock my door,
When I lay in a corner,
In utter grief.
Like heavy rain on the withered land,
Come to my arid heart,
With sweet cool breeze.

Nay, in my hours of rapture too,
When I kiss my nymph,
Or play with flowers of Nancy.
You share my delight,
And give a beam of light,
To enrich my fancy.

Or when I rest on the grass,
With stoic calmity,
And comfort.
O' muse I, with the sweet incense of life,
To make an offering to thee,
Crave thy presence into my idler heart.

– (December' 1988)

# On Talking To The Portrait Of My Love

Here is the portrait of my love –
What a sweet smile!
To reveal life,
And all my doubts about exile.

What petalous lips!
As if they utter the song divine.
I hear not,
In the greatest shrine.

Here is the portrait of my dove –
What an innocent look!
Yes, to give me light and strength,
More of the holiest book.

Ureka! Ureka! thou are truth O' beauty,
Yes, the truth lies here and herein beauty.

– (December' 1990)

# Spectrum Of Religion

Religion is like a beam of white light,
When passes through a prism ignorant.
Appears in the form of a spectrum, we note,
Buddha and Christ with colours different.

And when it shatters the glass,
We find the white radiance of eternity.
They mingle together VIBGYOR,
Into a single divinity.

– (December 1990)

## Lines Written In 1993

O' Life! Keep thy lute silent,
Strike it not again.
It is broken and,
Like a dirge it's music I hear in vain.

O' baby toys,
Allure me not further, go.
Your frail existence,
Alas, I did not know.

Like a fallen leaf,
I flatter in the void vast.
Dream and dream you can dream,
But alas, you don't know.

Weave and Weave a multicoloured web,
You can weave.
But forget not, yes forget not,
Nectar in a sieve!

What you think! What you say!
O' idler smart!
Truth of the leaf, Turth of the drop,
Will never die, say in short.

– (December' 1993)

## Doctors From Chancer To Present

"For gold in physique is cordial,
So, he loved it in special,"
Said the chancer centuries before,
Yet it needs to write more.

Why should he care for patients' bills,
To torture himself and make him ill?
Patients die – they die in the plural,
Let them die, death is natural.

Cry of the mourners deviate him not,
Brave is he, lamentation what?
Dirge he hears but like a Carol,
And burning pyres like Candles of balls.

A Doctor is he but first a human,
The pleasure of clubs – wit, wine and woman!
To this, he needs a salary unique,
Yes, a doctor is he – Doctor of Physique.

– (December 1993)

# Melpomene

I lay in sorrow,
Fear'd frustrated and futile.
On the bank of a river,
Tired, tame and sterile.

I could listen to the dirge,
Dirge from the fields and forest around.
Dirge from the sand and shrinking river,
Dirge from the Fox, Wolf and Hound.

Behold! the 'BRUTAS'
On the heap of corpses,
Decked with thorns,
And thorny foxes.

See, see, the blood,
Blood drops on the dew.
Blood on the clouds,
Blood on the hue.

Blood! Blood! Blood!
It oozes from roots.
Blood all around,
It oozes from shoots.

My heart bewilders,
I wake or dream.
Tumultuous is the scene,
And tumultuous scream.

Save Melpomene!
O' Goddess of the tragic arena.
Save the earth from Brutas vile,
Save the human endangered while.

– (June 1999)

## Lines Written In February 2009

You are restless today,
I do not know why? for the sake of desires unfulfilled?
Or for the sake of a goal unachieved?
Tell me the truth,
I am here in the hours of dejection.

You mute with tears in your eyes,
And lips unmoved,
Will not whisper a word I know,
Yet I am here,
In your hours of dejection.

Like a bird un-feathered in the forest green,
Watches soaring others in the skies,
Or deer wounded in the grass gazes.
Jumping others in the plains,
Grieve not I'm here in the hours of dejection.

I remember those hours,
When you and I would sit together,
In the oasis and you forget,
Your long toil amidst gentle breezes,
Blowing there, don't you remember?

You would say, "The oasis is lovely,
Yes, it is lovely,
Because of the vast desert around"
Once again I'm here,
In your hours of dejection.

Rejoice, rejoice friend,
Rejoice once again.
I fetch feathers for the un-feathered ones,
And fetch a drop of nectar,
To the wounds to heal.

Therefore my friend grieve not,
I'm here in your hours of dejection.

– (February' 2009)

# On The Path Of Lover

## I

What is thy goal maiden, to whom thou seek restlessly?

Endless ocean – Thou walk on the breakers with a garland of
precious, pearls in thy tender hands, who'll thou adore?

Thy cheeks are turning red, they spread the Carol thy lips
and thy eyes gaze in the silence, who do thou seek?

A green, green beach where sings the cuckoo her melodious
songs, thou keep thy pace on the swirling grass bearing a
handful odourous petals, whom thou adore?

Thy cheeks, soaked with serein reveal the secret thou
preserve, in thy heart. Tell me maiden who do thou seek?

- (July' 2009)

## II

A solitude – thou sit still on a rock with eyes shut and thy petalous lips murmur in the silence, whom do thou wish before thy eyes?

Lo! A flow of tears from thy eyes, perhaps to cool thy burning heart, whom do you seek O' virgin? on the cliff of a hill – near the clouds, thou sing thy songs of pipe, who do thou call?

Thy songs melodious vibrate the skies and its echo is hear'd in the heavens, yet no one answers thee, who do thou seek?

Fall of snow – thou still walk, thy feet skip and stumble, yet ye stand erect and move further. Such is thy love!

– (July 2009)

## III

Dense, dense fog – thy path not visible to make thee bewilder thy face turns pale and hair locks, spread yet thou linger not, such is thy love!

A thorny forest – thou walk on the thorns and bleed thy feet, yet thou wipe thy tears and smile in the silence, such is thy pleasure!

A dark, dark valley – A devil on thy path to devour thy sweet existence, yet ye tremble not and with eyes shut combat him, he touches ye not, such is thy faith!

– (July' 2009)

## IV

A wide desert – the warmth of the sun to char thy face and sandy winds to spoil thy brocade. Not a drop of water to drench thy throat nor a single shower of sea breeze, yet thou brake not thy Journey and reach to an Oasis.

A swirling fountain, a boon to thy weariness, thou sit by and ask, "What is thy destination O' fountain?", It whispers something in the silence, to make thee smile and thou proceed.

O' maid immortal! immortal is, thy love and thy songs divine, but tell me maiden where doth finish thy Journey?

– (July 2009)

## V

Endless is thy journey O' immortal Nymph! Open thy eyes and come out of thy dream. Rejoice, Rejoice O' maiden for he is already with thee to whom thou seek restlessly.

Never leaves thee alone and restless is he too to seek thy love and with arms expanded stands at thee and spread his lips sweet shower of a smile. Such is thy lover and thou poor virgin gaze towards the skies in interrogation.

When thou blow thy pipe gazing towards the horizon, thy songs of dirge utter the tale of thy aching heart and thou shed tears to lessen thy grief. Then thy lover whispers at thy ears sitting beside thee and yet thou unfortunate gaze towards the skies in interrogation.

– (July 2009)

## VI

Melancholy swims on thy lips, thee bewilder and fall on the ground, thy lover soothes thee, decorates thy hair entangled and doth bring a sweet shower serein to make you fresh and fine. Such is thy lover!

Thou sit in a corner with eyes shut and keep the image of thy lover into thy heart, he knocks thy door at once and ye dove murmur, “Let the image of my lover not escape out of my temple”, he smiles at thy answer. Such is the chemistry of your love!

Thus thou travel and travel since the first ray of the sun illuminated the earth, when’ll thou finish thy Journey O’ maiden!

- (July’ 2009)

## VII

When thou rest beneath a tree fresh and flowered, craves thy heart the arms of thy Lover, then decks thy bosom sweet shower of petals at once. Such is the pleasure of thy lover!

Ages passed since thou seek thy lover, yet thee find him not. He still smiles and stands with arms expanded to embrace thee and thy heart, yet ye poor dove Coy and dream!

Stop dreaming maiden, put thy veil aside, coy not and give thy arms in the arms of thy Lover for he craves a rapturous moment with thee. What a lover is he and thy love O' maiden!

– (July' 2009)

## VIII

The winds are lovely and calm blowing and they deck thy petalous cheeks the pearly droplets of the breakers. Thus thou walk on the breakers high where sings the lark the songs of thy heart.

Do ye notice, O' maiden!

But take care, O' maiden, the shark is ready beneath thy feet to devour thy sweet existence. Walk, walk, O' maiden ever walk in the search of thy lover but forget not that you are seated between Lark on the head and the Shark beneath, beneath thy feet.

Take care O' maiden!

Sing, Sing, O' maiden the songs of rapture with the lovely lark and never permit the ugly shark to spoil thy brocade, not easy is the combat!

– (July' 2009)

## IX

The Lark doth sing and still sing the song of rapture, song of thy heart. Do you hear the flutter of her plumes which make harmony with thy rhythm of life? Listen to it with care, full of help to find thy lover!

The Lark doth sing and still sing, thou praise her song and proceed. The shark beneath the feet doth try to devour thee, thou kick him and proceed. Thy lover craves the nectar of thy lips, thou open not thy eyes, stand still and coy O' dove. Great is thy lover and greater is thy love, O' sweet maiden!

– (July' 2009)

## The Creator

Who made the sky?
The sustainer of all –
The earth, the water,
The fire and the air.

Who motivates the planets,
And stars to move with duty-bound freedom.
And gives disciplined motion,
Electrons and protons in every atom.

Who motivates the cell,
To divide and grow faster.
To make a blade of grass,
And the body of a man or a monster.

Thus we see the matter,
Matter overall.
Living and non–living,
Big and small.

Thus we see,
The Moon, The Sun and other stars.
And the earth with water, wind and fire,
Bearing incense and twitter everywhere near and far.

Thus we see the hue,
From algae to angiosperms.
And more advanced,
Euglena to the elephants.

But who knows,
This secret of the Creator.
No one except the man,
The best creation of its maker.

Yes, It is the man,
Who knows that he knows better.
And thus he seeks the self,
And it's maker.

He finds the self,
In the form of divine soul.
And his maker,
In the form of the Soul of the souls.

Thus there is the God,
The God is there without doubt.
Utter every cell of my body,
The God is there without doubt.

What do you think, O' Man!

I know not.

Eureka! Eureka!

Overjoyed am I, I got.

– (December 2012)

## Lines Written On The Eve Of Retirement

What though the sixty two,
Summers of my life have,
Passed and sixty two winters.

All is not passed –
Silver twitter and golden,
Silence of a teacher.

I'm a maker of the man –
The Bureaucrat, the Technocrat,
The Parliamentarian, and all!

I'm the seeker of the truth,
Roaming in the void,
Amidst the big and small.

Immortal is the Soul,
It gains a body again;
Then in the next,
I would like to be,
known as a teacher,
Yes, would like to be known as a teacher!

– (30th June 2020)

## My Dear Companion Soul

I, alone in the mortal planet of the Universe, seek my companion soul, gazing towards the sky among the Pleiades in interrogation.

Here, she lives; here, she dwells; here, she wanders now with other blessed souls in the blissful Empire of God-seeking a sacred throne for me too, in the fit of affection.

She is no more with me with her physical existence, but her divine soul comes and goes to make a bridge between the two to maintain the immortal relationship.

Immortal, we are two loving souls and Immortal, is our love, utter my breaths and thus, inhale and exhale I mundane to seek the satiety in sedation.

Two atoms of oxygen create a bond to make a molecule divine and so is the chemistry of our loving souls to make a molecule with full satiety and saturation.

Thus, a molecule of two loving souls hiding a great deal of divine energy floats and flourish, rejoices and reigns, in the heavens high and in extreme gets salvation.

– (May 2021)

9 789357 044226

Printed by Libri Plureos GmbH in Hamburg,
Germany